Trientrepreneur

A Trient Press Publication for Authors & Entrepreneurs

$10.99

Trient Press

Copyright © 2021 by Trient Press

All rights reserved. No part of this book may be reproduced or used in any manner without written permission of the copyright owner except for the use of quotations in a book review. For more information, address: info@trientpress.com

FIRST EDITION

www.trientpressmagazine.com

From Trient Press

> "This is a great book for those who like suspense, great detail and unforgettable writing!

Suspense around every corner

06 Shirred eggs

07 Chicken Wraps

09 May Author Tips

10 For the New Starters

15 Author Interviews:

 R.B Carr, Claerie Kavanaugh and Thresa Corbley Siller

23 From Rags to Riches

TRIENTREPRENEUR
ISSUE 2

28 Say "Yes," to Less

30 Lets Talk Mentors

33 Rock Your Audiance

38 The Naked Truth

42 Explore, Thrive, Expand

44 Resources for New Authors

46 Resources for Entrepreneurs

PERFECTING THE IDEAL
SHIRRED EGGS

Also known as baked eggs, it is a dish in which eggs have been baked in a flat-bottomed dish; the name originates from the type of dish in which it was traditionally baked. An alternative way of cooking is to crack the eggs into individual ramekins and cook them in a water bath, creating the French dish eggs.

By: Melisa Ruscsak
Photo: Shutter Stock

Ingredients:

- 1/4 teaspoon softened butter
- 2 teaspoons heavy cream
- 2 eggs
- salt and pepper to taste
- 1 teaspoon minced fresh chives
- 1 teaspoon grated Parmesan cheese

Directions:

- Ready the center of the ramekin, then sprinkle with salt, pepper, chives, and Parmesan cheese. Pour cream into the ramekin, then crack the eggs on top of the cream without breaking the yolks. Use a spoon to position the yolks towards the center.

- Bake in preheated oven until the whites of the eggs have set and the yolks are still soft, 12 to 15 minutes. Remove from oven, and allow to set for 2 to 3 minutes before serving.

SIMPLE Chicken Wraps

by: Melisa Ruscsak

Ingredients:
- 1 package of Chicken Tenderloins
- 12oz Bacon
- Shredded Lettuce
- Mozzarella Cheese
- 1 package of Tortillas
- Paprika
- BBQ Seasoning
- BBQ Sauce
- ½ c Mayo

Directions:

Preheat oven to 350 degrees
On a sheet tray, place chicken tenderloins. Sprinkle with seasoning. Bake for 15 min.
Cook bacon until crisp. Let cool, then crumble. Add mayo and mix. Set in fridge until ready to use.
On the stove heat BBQ sauce until liquid.
Dredge, Chicken in BBQ sauce, then cook for another 5 min. Repeat until chicken is done.

On tortilla shells spread mayo mixture. Add lettuce and cheese. Place Chicken on top, then roll up folding the bottom up, but leave the top open.

Great paired with fries, tots or rice.

MAY AUTHOR TIPS

Writing tips for beginners:

- Read a lot. Read stuff that's similar to what you'd like to write and then read stuff that's more literary too.
- Write about what you know. It's a cliché, but it's true.
- Have your own voice. Practice not sounding like everyone else.
- Take a creative writing course.
- Decide on a genre. We often write best, what we love to read.
- Write the ending first.
- Do a first draft. Then, write a second and third draft.
- Don't be afraid to self-edit.
- If you are writing dialogue, say it aloud as you type it. If it sounds like writing, rewrite it.

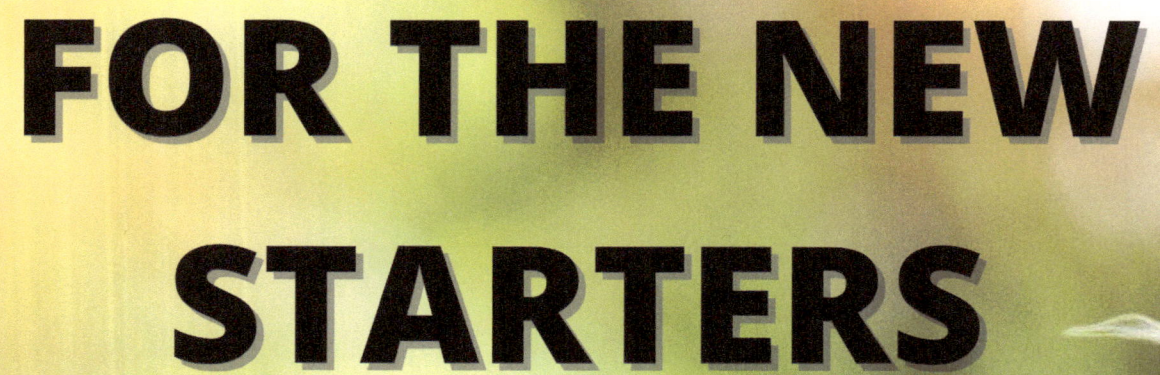

FOR THE NEW STARTERS

TRIENT PRESS MAGAZINE　　　　　MAY 2021

FOR THE NEW STARTERS

BY USAMA HUSSAIN

Entrepreneurship is one of the most fascinating and attractive professions for many youngsters and those who love taking risks. The term Entrepreneurship received good traction in the 20th century while it has a long history.

The Entrepreneurial proclivity can be observed in every era since ancient times however the 20th and 21st centuries are its golden ages as it got worldwide recognition. Entrepreneurship is a profession that changes the destiny of many young and dedicated businessmen, but it can subvert the situation for many others. If not taken with the solemnity it can make billionaires bankrupts. This is the fun and joy that lies in Entrepreneurship, an uncertain dilemma that is easy to tackle if treated wisely, courageously, patiently, and smartly.

Entrepreneurs invest their money or owe money to start a business and then escalate it, many of them sustain in the market, many failed while few excel. Those who excel earned name and fame fortnightly, while those who fail might suffer a lot and many give up while many others learn from their failure and start again enthusiastically with zeal and ebullition. Chances are gravid for those who want to recover if they articipate. Successful Entrepreneurs inspire others through their stories. There are many real-life examples of successful Entrepreneurs who win the game at a very early stage like Bill Gates who become the world's richest person at 30.

In addition, there are those who started at old age like Colonel Sander founder of KFC. Many others like Jeff Bezos, Jack Ma, and many others. Everyone has his or her own fable and a lesson to teach new Entrepreneurs. Their journey was not easy but they never loosed hearts and stand with a more zealous attitude as they suffer. Sometimes they failed completely but then they zoomed out the situation and analyze their mistakes, learn, relearn, and avoided those mistakes that led them to fail. They had learned from their failure and criticisms. Jack Ma the founding father of ALI BABA said once "you failed multiple times and succeeded one time" and Their journey was not easy but they never loosed hearts and stand with a more zealous attitude as they suffer. Sometimes they failed completely, but then they zoomed out the situation and analyze their mistakes, learn, relearn, and avoided those mistakes that led them to fail. They had learned from their failure and criticisms. Jack Ma the founding father of ALI BABA said once, "you failed multiple times and succeeded one time" and this one-time success defines you, it becomes your journey and your destiny and it's then your responsibility to maintain this success, and this distinguishes you from the rest of the world. This success becomes your identity and your brand for the entire life and onward.

Entrepreneurship does not require a genius mind, a large social circle, tons of money, and higher education, but it requires a brilliant idea, team spirit, broader view, leadership, tolerance, patience, and time management, maintaining standards, dutiful and honest attitude. Even an average person starts a business, but the one who struggles, suffers, and accepts challenges, takes the risk, and makes hard decisions. The journey that he decides makes him extraordinary. Every new starter faces many problems, which are sometimes bear out great hurdles and obstacles in their journey. Here we will address some such problem and their solutions.

CONFUSION ON DECIDING WHAT TO SELL:
Many of the new Entrepreneurs cannot decide what to sell. However, this is not important, important thing is to decide why you want to sell before what to sell. Once you find the why then you will easily find how to sell and then ultimately what to sell. Customers are not interested in your product they are interested in your why; they are seeking a solution of their need in your why, the answer to which is then your product.

THINKING IN SHORT TERM:
Every one of us wants immediate results, new business starters also desire to get immediate profit and growth for their business, which is not always possible. As a starter, you must be patient because great things take time and great results require great efforts. Do not set short-term goals only. Plan for the long term along with the necessary short term goals, but focus mostly on the long term. Think in a larger purview; expand your horizon and perspective. Always set high and realistic goals, focusing on the long term. Don't concentrate much on saving; focus on investing because investing always brings the best results. Improve your capital and work on your team if any.

"Small, consistent changes are the key to phenomenal long-term results."

COMPETITORS CHALLENGES AND MARKET STRATEGIES

Competitors might wreak hefty challenges, which need to be tackled wisely and smartly. An often starters indulge themselves in a comparison with their competitors which is not a solution but is another problem. You have to identify your customer's needs and the way you can bring them a solution. Try to build strong and long relations with your customers so that they do not ever try a substitute for your product because customer retention is very much important in today's competitive market. Instead of skirting your customers with ads and flowery words, try to educate them about your services and about your products. This is the most effective marketing strategy.

PERSPECTIVES

Change your habits and attitude, according to your customer's needs and wants. Research different ideas related to your business, study the habits and tactics of the most successful people Entrepreneurs related to your start-up. Try to figure out what strategies and tools they had used, it should be an effective way to grow your startup rapidly. Analyze your weakness, identify your mistakes and resolve your issues. Use technology and the internet effectively to grow your business. Social media can be the best tool in this regard.

Most of the new starters quit their business within the first three years because they do not consider the above-mentioned issues. Everyone faces problems and failures, but the only effective way is to learn from them and to go ahead.

INTERVIEW WITH R.B. CARR

LYNN: HOW DO YOU PROCESS AND DEAL WITH NEGATIVE BOOK REVIEWS?

R.B: I think you have to consider any criticism with a grain of salt. I don't like every best-selling book or hit movie that comes along and I very often disagree with critics regarding the same. I think you have to keep in mind that these reviews are subjective in that way. Some people are simply not going to like it.

As long as I am happy with my work, first and foremost and I enjoyed the process of developing the story and polishing the product, then I have no complaints. If some other people get enjoyment out of it than so much the better.

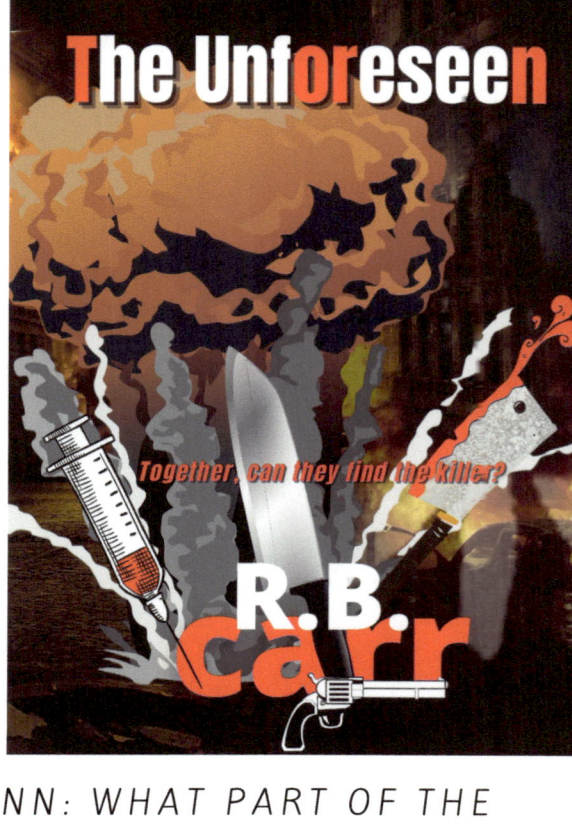

LYNN: WHAT ADVICE WOULD YOU GIVE TO A WRITER WORKING ON THEIR FIRST BOOK?

R.B: Write every day. Even if only a paragraph, write. Develop your craft and your story. It is all trial and error and no one writes their first draft to perfection, so anticipate you will be editing and changing things as you go, but keep moving the project forward.

LYNN: WHAT PART OF THE BOOK WAS THE MOST FUN TO WRITE?

R.B: I love the action scenes. Having grown up as a fan of comic books, Louis L'Amour novels, and 80's action movies, I am a big fan of fight scenes and like to bring my own creative twists to each and every one. And it is fun to come up with scenarios in which are novel. You can't simply let the book be dominated by gunshots to the head, it gets stale too quickly.

LYNN: WHAT'S YOUR FAVORITE WRITING SNACK OR DRINK?

R.B: COFFEE!!!!

LYNN: IF YOU'RE PLANNING A SEQUEL, CAN YOU SHARE A TINY BIT ABOUT YOUR PLANS FOR IT?

R.B: I am currently writing a sequel to The Unforeseen that will explore more of the relationship between Logan and Paige. Of course, that will be told within more mayhem when Logan is forced to put his skills as one of the premier contract killers to work in an effort to save Paige, his handler, from a group of mercenaries trying to collect a contract on her.

LYNN: IF YOU COULD SPEND A DAY WITH ANOTHER POPULAR AUTHOR, WHOM WOULD YOU CHOOSE?

R.B. : Without a doubt, Micheal Connelly, who I think is one of the best storytellers there is. His characters, plot lines, and his prose are simply some of the best there is today. I would love to pick his brain about style and how he developed characters such as Harry Bosch or the Lincoln Lawyer.

LYNN: WHAT IS THE MOST VALUABLE PIECE OF ADVICE YOU'VE BEEN GIVEN ABOUT WRITING?

R.B. : Don't be afraid of the delete button. Sometimes you are going to have an idea or scenario that simply doesn't fit in the story or picture you are trying to write. Even good ones sometimes need to be omitted to better tell the overall story.

LYNN: WHAT DO YOU THINK IS THE BEST WAY TO IMPROVE WRITING SKILLS?

R.B: Like any skill, practice, practice, and practice. And don't be afraid to hear or accept coaching and criticism.

LYNN: HOW DO YOU COME UP WITH CHARACTER NAMES FOR YOUR STORIES?

R,B.: Most of my character names are based upon people I am acquainted with in some form or fashion. Often times they are named as such because of some character trait those people have that I want to use within a story, though oftentimes the characters are spun beyond recognition by the time the work is done. To me, it is easier to keep track of people and characters I know than to come up with them completely out of thin air.

LYNN: WHOM DO YOU TRUST FOR OBJECTIVE AND CONSTRUCTIVE CRITICISM OF YOUR WORK?

R.B : I have three friends that preview my work. I know all three will be unabashed in offering criticism. As importantly, none of the three are acquainted so I know their feedback is not groupthink. If two, or worse yet, all three, point out the same flaw in something, I know for sure it isn't simply some subjective discrepancy.

To read the full interview, please visit us at https://trientpressmagazine.com/

INTERVIEW

CLAERIE KAVANAUGH
Author Interview

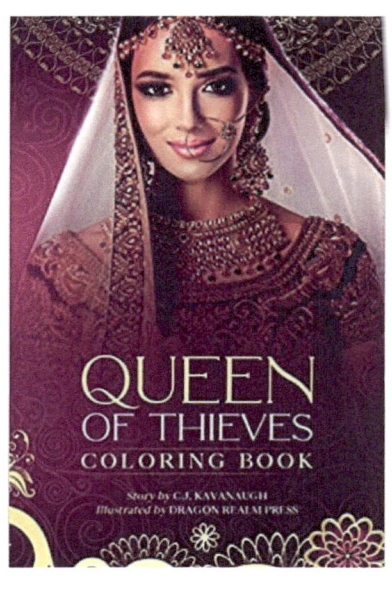

LYNN: WHAT IS THE MOST DIFFICULT PART OF YOUR WRITING PROCESS?

Claerie: I think the most difficult part for me is actually the first shift. What most people would probably consider a zero draft is what my outline looks like. They're often between 10 to 15 pages and they're super detailed because I am a planner to the core. But at the same time, because I know exactly what needs to happen, it sometimes feels like I've already written the story by the time I get to drafting it. My favorite part is actually the editing. It's not a coincidence that that's also my day job :-) but I enjoy editing my own work because I have something to work with and now it's my job to make it as engaging for my readers as possible.

LYNN: WHAT ARE COMMON TRAPS FOR NEW AUTHORS?

Claerie: Don't focus on Perfection. Don't even aim for it. There's no such thing as a perfect book. You're never going to please everyone and the only person you need to worry about pleasing, especially if you're new, is yourself. If you're happy with the book then the odds are someone else will be too.

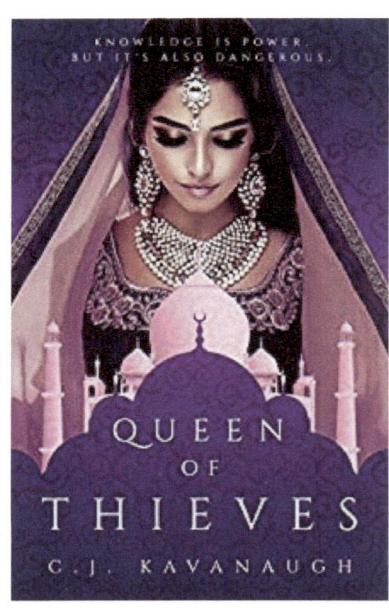

LYNN: WHAT COMES FIRST FOR YOU — THE PLOT OR THE CHARACTERS — AND WHY?

Claerie: This is a trim question for me because prior to writing the book that I'm working on now the answer absolutely definitely would have been the plot comes first and then I pick the characters that are going to work best within that plot. A lot of the time, the characters and the plot come to me simultaneously especially because I prefer to do retellings or put a spin on something I'm already a little bit familiar with. But with the book that I'm working on now, I knew what I wanted to scene to be and I knew who the main character was and I knew what season I wanted it to take place in, but that was pretty much it. I had to build the plot backwards and that was an entirely new experience for me. It was a fun one, but let's just say for future books I hope that my muse goes back to giving me the plot before I get characters.

LYNN; HOW MANY BOOKS HAVE YOU WRITTEN AND WHICH IS YOUR FAVORITE?

Claerie: By the time this may or may not be published the answer will be four, which is kind of crazy. Which book is my favorite? That's like asking me who is my favorite pet or sibling!

Just kidding! I think my favorite book is always going to be the one I'm currently working on because I hope that I grow as a writer with every single book. So far, every project I worked on has taught me something different and this one is no exception.

LYNN: WHAT ADVICE WOULD YOU GIVE TO A WRITER WORKING ON THEIR FIRST BOOK?

Claerie: Focus on the story and have fun with it. Don't worry too much about what you're going to do with it until you have at least a first draft completed. I definitely made that mistake, not only with my first, but also with the books that I tried to write after I published my first book. In fact, a couple of months ago, I recently went through a period where I didn't feel like writing at all because the stress of what I was going to do after I wrote the book was really getting to me. Had to alter my mindset and remind myself that above all this is supposed to be something I do for fun. Yes, I hope to make some money off of it one day, but I wouldn't be doing it at all if I didn't enjoy it. So have fun and embrace the process.

LYNN: IF YOU WERE TO WRITE A SPIN-OFF ABOUT A SIDE CHARACTER, WHICH WOULD YOU PICK?

Claerie: Had to answer this question because it kind of made me laugh. The series that I'm working on right now is actually a spin-off. In a LGBTQ romance book that I wrote in 2017 and published in 2019, one of the characters has a daughter and that's the character we follow in the current series I'm working on, called Lyssa's Holiday Hyjinks. Even though they take place in the same world, they're completely different stories that can be read without ever touching the other if you don't want to. One is a contemporary romance and the other is a middle grade contemporary fantasy. .

LYNN: IF YOU'RE PLANNING A SEQUEL, CAN YOU SHARE A TINY BIT ABOUT YOUR PLANS FOR IT?

Claerie: Providing that the series does as well as I hope it will do, and actually planning many many Sikh world! The whole concept behind the series is that they're all connected because they all feature the same main character, but they're completely separate stories.

In each book, the main character somehow comes across a mythical creature and it centers around a particular holiday. The main character has to help that mythical creature get back to where they came from and learns a lesson in the process. Usually the lesson has something to do with the holiday, but not always. I don't want to give away anything specific about the next book because I don't know when this will be published yet but I will say that if one of your favorite mythical creatures is featured around the holiday, you might very well see them in this series.

LYNN: WHAT BOOKS DID YOU GROW UP READING?

Claerie: I grew up reading the Magic Tree House, Percy Jackson, and one of my absolute favorite series is A Great and Terrible Beauty Trilogy by Libba Bray.

LYNN: NAME AN UNDERAPPRECIATED NOVEL THAT YOU LOVE.

Claerie: I feel like nobody talks about A Great and Terrible Beauty Trilogy by Libba Bray anymore and I don't understand why. I feel like her writing is so immersive and I wish more people knew about it.

LYNN: WHAT DO THE WORDS "LITERARY SUCCESS" MEAN TO YOU? HOW DO YOU PICTURE IT?

Claerie: Literary success doesn't necessarily mean making it onto any big lists or even making a full-time living with my work. It means making enough money off of my writing to take my family on an awesome trip or two a couple times a year and having a community of people that enjoy my work and can't wait for the next one. Community is more important than money to me especially in this case.

LYNN: WHAT IS A SIGNIFICANT WAY YOUR BOOK HAS CHANGED SINCE THE FIRST DRAFT?

Claerie: Oh my goodness! So, in order to get a little bit more specific for this question I'm going to talk about the first book in the series, which is coming out in September!

The craziest thing is the entire idea for this series came from one throw away line in an entirely different book of mine. It was about a ghost that had haunted a ballet school. I know I didn't do ballet but I was a theater kid for most of my life. In theater, there are plenty of superstitions and ghost stories to keep a creative mind wondering. The thing that changes the most from the first batch to the final draft of that book was honestly the entire relationship between the main character and the ghost. I can't say anything specific, 'cause I don't want spoilers, but it took a lot of rewriting.

To read the full interview, please visit us at:
https://trientpressmagazine.com/

Must be something dead out there'

> "First hand knowledge of investigative procedures is evident from the first to the last suspense filled pages. He lives in Las Vegas.

GRADY HARPE

Customer Review

Can There Be Hope For A Compulsive Overeater?

BY: THERESA CORBLEY SILLER

Angela stuffed her large girth into the booth at the sports bar and grill, and smiled at her friends. She was thrilled it was Friday night, and she could relax and enjoy a drink and some appetizers with the gang. As they all caught up with each other's lives, the artichoke dip/chips, chili cheese fries and pizza bites arrived. Sipping her beer, she couldn't wait until that first bite of lusciousness bombarded her senses with pleasure.

As they all joked and laughed together, Angela was dismayed to notice that she had scarfed down more than her fair share of pizza bites. The server returned, eyeing the almost-empty plate and asked, "Do you all want me to bring out more of those?"

Angela looked sheepish as she answered, "Uh...yes please. Sorry guys, I guess I just got carried away." It was always the same scenario, every single time she went to Happy Hour with her group.

The other ladies sipped their drinks, munched on the appetizers for a bit, then seemed to be comfortably satiated as they pushed their plates away. Angela was appalled at the way the yummy snacks quickly disappeared once she got started. She always grabbed one last chip as she shimmied her rotund frame out of the booth, shouldered her purse, said her goodbyes and headed out the door.

When she got home from this nosh-fest, she made herself a full dinner. None of the food ever seemed to satisfy her completely. Angela topped off her Friday nights with a movie and a half gallon of ice cream.

Saturday mornings the self-loathing commenced. So uncomfortably bloated, she waddled over to her bathroom scale, stepped up and covered her eyes. One little peek and her misgivings were confirmed. She, of the 5' 2" frame, tipped the scales at 315 pounds. She looked at herself in the mirror, fearing how much more she'd blow up, in her lifetime.

"Next time we go to Happy Hour I'll only have a little," she promised herself. "Maybe I could start on a new diet Monday morning." She researched online the juice-cleanse diets where she could lose weight quickly.

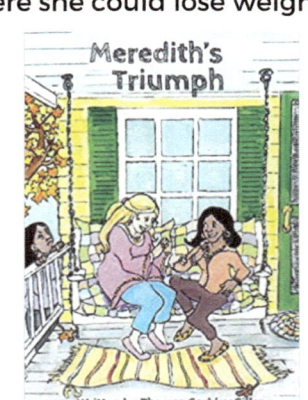

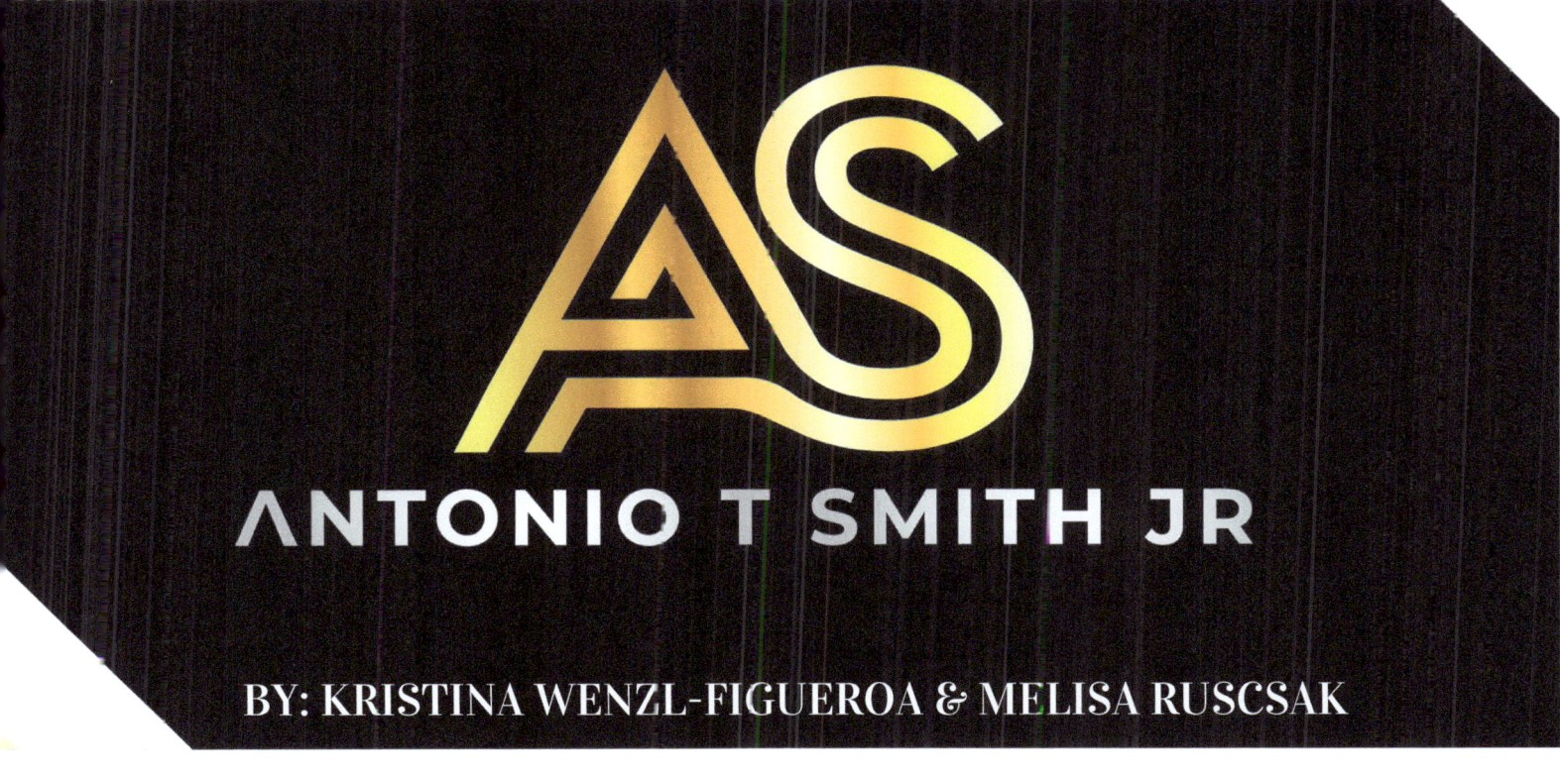

BY: KRISTINA WENZL-FIGUEROA & MELISA RUSCSAK

From Rags to Riches

In life we talk about mentors, we talk about how our teachers, business owners, and our friends and family have mentored us. Now, I would like to introduce you to a man who's not only a great mentor to myself but is a world-renowned business coach, life coach, mentor, entrepreneur, and much more. ATS Jr. Companies along with his other endeavors gives this individual a net worth of over two hundred and fifty million dollars and aligns him to be one of the world's billionaires by 2025.

Now, before I give you his name let me tell you a little about him. This man, this mentor and coach who we see as a great influence on today's society, did not start at the top. He did not start by setting out to be a mentor, coach, or entrepreneur--he's simply set out to survive.

I had the pleasure of meeting this man a few years ago when he had just published his third book, or was in the process of publishing his third book, in which he outlined steps to overcome poverty based on his experience. This man who as a child started out homeless and sleeping in a dumpster, has gone on to become an inspiration and a mentor to so many. His name is Antonio T. Smith, Jr., and this is his story.

At six years old, Antonio was living on the streets of Galveston, Texas, going to school at the local elementary school just to have a hot meal at least once a day. This man recognized as a child, the importance of an education and prioritized going, amidst adversity that would have otherwise rendered so many paralysed by their misfortune and circumstance.

Eventually CPS caught wind of his situation and he was bounced from home to home until he was adopted at the age of fourteen. He pushed himself to continue attending high school where he learned the art of side-hustling, doing what he deemed was required in order to survive.

After high school he was faced with a decision--go to work at a fast-food place and work 9-5, or serve in the military. Antonio chose to gain valuable life experience from serving in the United States Army, which gave him a taste of what hard work and determination could do for him.

Following his service in the Army, he returned to Galveston and as a minister, mentored and helped as many people as he could.

This desire to help others slowly grew into the empire he has created, a vast network of other entrepreneurs and motivational coaches who teach others to become motivational coaches. ATS Jr. Companies teach other CEOs and entrepreneurs how to run their companies and to not only to help themselves, but to help others by creating jobs and environments that people want to work in.

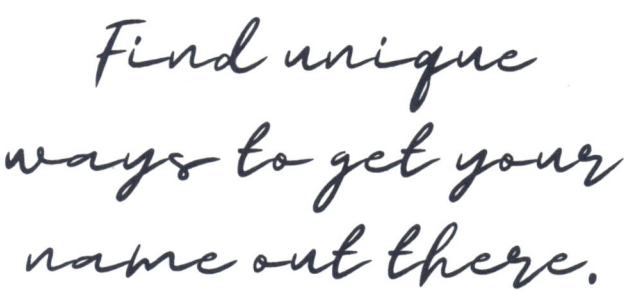

Find unique ways to get your name out there.

Antonio coaches about topics like Guerilla Marketing--finding unique ways to get your name out there. He suggests things like creating apparel with your logo on it, or writing a book. He encourages entrepreneurs to follow viral trends and to partner with local businesses. He even recognizes the untapped potential kids have to sell products, which in many instances works into the guerilla marketing plan he teaches his mentees to use. There are so many marketing tips Antonio has discovered, which he shares when talks business, but most of all, the message he wants to get across in his teachings is to be creative in how you market to your followers.

Through all of this, Antonio's main mission has been to help others escape poverty. His main desire is to break people free from the bonds of their 9 to 5 jobs, from making minimum wage, and from the poverty-bound brain that whispers to them that this is all they'll ever be, and instead sets them on the path to making them millionaires. I know it sounds a little crazy to think about a millionaire wanting to give away wealth, yet this is his mission. Antonio T. Smith, Jr. wants to spread the wealth through the teachings on his professional website: https://theatsjr.thinkific.com/

His company has coursework that ranges from free/month to $49/month, to help people achieve not only becoming entrepreneurs and motivational speakers, but pillars of their communities, who in turn raise the less fortunate from their poverty-bound mindsets.

In addition to his coursework, Antonio is a popular podcast host, with a total of 12 podcast shows that reach 70 countries, in 60 different languages and he has a following and network of over 2.3 million people world wide. Antonio T. Smith, Jr. is the CEO of the #1 online millionaire training academy in the world, the ATS Business University. Antonio is also the CEO of the fastest growing network marketing company in the world and is disrupting the network marketing industry with The ATS Network. Through this network, he has taken the #1 online millionaire training academy in the world and created a way for members to earn while they are learning how to make their businesses and brands more profitable and through this company, he is fulfilling his mission of creating 100,000 millionaires. The ATS Network has grown exponentially in just a few short years, with international offices, the latest one that opened in Ethiopia.

Antonio is an internationally recognized trainer, speaker, and is a five time best-selling author in religious and self-help categories. Antonio has several books currently available, his first: Keep Walking, to his latest: 18 Steps to Excellence, most of which have reached the Amazon Best Seller List in the United States and globally. He specializes in Cognitive Behavior Therapy, Business and Strength Training, Leadership, Teleconference Presentations, Personal Breakthroughs, Prosperity Consciousness, Mindset Training, and all levels of effective marketing, as well as scholarship in the Old Testament and Jewish Covenants, and he owns one of the most successful technology companies in Texas. He holds a bachelor's in Christianity and a Master's in Theological Studies from Houston Baptist University.

Antonio T. Smith, Jr. has mentored. He has taught the misfortunate and downtrodden to take charge of their lives. He has inspired and encouraged individuals to reach for greatness.

Antonio has created a brand, he has created wealth, and he has created ever-lasting partnerships with people such as Brad Blazar and others who succeed by helping others succeed. This is the legacy that Antonio T. Smith, Jr. has created, and those who he has mentored, coached, and presided over as a minister--thank him from the bottom of their hearts.

Use the link below to get his free book that gives you all the secrets Antonio learned to exit the middle-class and get into the top 1% and start taking steps to your future.
https://therichestmaninthetrashcan.com/

https://theatsjr.thinkific.com/users/checkout/auth
https://www.facebook.com/theatsjr
https://www.linkedin.com/in/antoniotsmithjr/
SUPPORT ON PATREON:
https://www.patreon.com/theatsjr
Shoot him a text at +1 409-500-1546

BREAK THE SILENCE. BREAK THE CHAINS.

HELP STOP HUMAN TRAFFICKING

Join the fight at humantraffickinghotline.org

TRIENT PRESS MAGAZINE ADVICE COLUMN

SAY "YES," TO LESS

BY: KRISTINA WENZL-FIGUEROA

In today's world where each of us wears many hats, it is often difficult to know how to navigate the demands of everyday life. I know for me personally, I am Wife, Friend, Mother, Daughter, Sister, Teacher, Writer, Chief Operating Officer, Business Partner, Cheerleader, Cook, Personal Assistant, Office Manager... and the list truly goes on. It's not even that I consciously chose to wear this many hats—sure, some I gladly took on knowing the time-cost and commitment—but other's just sort of landed on my head.

I am sure many of you can relate, and this is even after I've read the book, "The Best Yes," by Lysa TerKeurst, a book about making wise decisions in the midst of endless demands.

Maybe I'm just a hat collector?

In all seriousness, why do we take on more than we knowingly can do well? NOT that I am failing at any of my roles, but certainly we all strive for perfection and to excel at what we do, right? So then why the compulsion to take on EVERYTHING at the risk that what we are doing will leave us exhausted, moody, and underwhelmed about the achievements and accomplishments of those who mean the most to us?

Instead of saying yes to it all, maybe it would make more sense to say yes to a little less? Is it enormously important for me to make every fieldtrip my child goes on, or to bring snack for every game? Is it really my role to edit every friend's book that comes across my desk—even when they are already paying for an editor? Do I really need to launder and iron my clothing instead of taking it to the dry cleaners or bake homemade desserts and keep the house spotless?

NO.

You don't have to be a superhuman to be loved, accepted, acknowledged, or respected.

It's okay to strip off your hats and say to the world—**This is me!**—because you are enough, being just you...imperfect, sweatpants wearing, messy-bun...

YOU.

It's okay to let other people take over some of the many hats that you wear—and it's okay for me to shed some of my own as well.

Sometimes we just need to be reminded that **WE** matter. That what **WE** need is also a priority, and once we take the time to find our inner balance and what centers us—then doing everything else we choose to take on, becomes that much easier and rewarding.

So, for all of you who can relate to what I'm putting out there, I encourage you to start small and find five or ten minutes a day where you can meditate, reflect and truly question what it is that makes you most happy. I guarantee it isn't having spotless toilet bowls or being able to be called "best-friend" by the PTA President.

I would wager the things that make you happiest are the people that you wish you could spend more time with—quality time with. Maybe it's your spouse, your sibling, your friend or children who have accidentally gone by the wayside while you were making sure they saw you in your best clothes and in your cleanest home.

I encourage you to reevaluate your priorities to include yourself and to accept that being you—the real, less than perfect you—IS ENOUGH.

Kristina Wenzl-Figuerca is a full-time business owner, entrepreneur, and homeschooling stay-at-home mom. She loves to write and has several contemporary and adult romances under the pen name, Tina Maurine. You can like and follow her on Facebook, Instagram and Twitter under her pen name or visit her website for more information on her books.
https://tinamaurine.com/

M.I. Ruscsak

Lets Talk Mentors

by: Melisa Ruscsak

If you ask a CEO of a company how they got to the position they are today , most will say hard work and determination. Yet a few will be honest and give a key tip, they will say that they had a mentor, a coach or other form of key person in their life that showed them how to succeed. The will mention that teacher, sports coach, pastor , or even a family member that inspired them to reach for their goals. These are the Ceo's that have raised up through diversity and hardship to create empires. These are the Ceo's that reach out and mentor the next generation of entrepreneurs.

Now, I know if you search business coaches you will find at least ten pages of coaches. All of them good, all of them trained with a mindset to help you grow. Yet merely reaching out and listing will not help you or your company grow. Doing countless worksheets , talking problems out, and trouble shooting won't matter until you do one think for yourself….

I... you must have the mindset to succeed.

I won't matter how the cards are stacked against you. Won't matter if you have to work a day job while building your dreams. First you need the mindset, then you need a business mentor.

Mindset coaches are there but only if you are truly ready. You can pay hundreds of dollars. Buy countless books. Waist months or years going yeah I listened to.... read books buy.... but nothing worked. Or stand there and say I don't have time to listen to some coach.

Yet we do listen. In short burst when no one is paying attention. We watch video's on social media. Hear coaches and mentors on the radio. Watch them on t.v in the most unlikely places. And we slowly learn little things. Soon we will tune in to key words. Mentor, coaches, those who inspired and believed in the person we find ourselves following.

Now we are ready for the next step. Now we are ready to reprogram our minds to succeed. The burning to be more than we are is starting to take shape. Yet we need someone to counter all of the negative we have heard before now. We need some one who can identify our fear and help us over come it.

This is the moment we start to follow our chosen mentors. Seek them out on sites like LinkedIn, and Instagram. Follow them for their free advice. Not yet ready to go all in, yet we earn to raise above where we are now. We are at the turning point now... stay where we are or rise above.

We seek out the mentors. Read the books that resonate within us. Seek out those who have risen over diversity. We start to see that their rise to riches took years not months. We understand the long nights, working two jobs and still working their business. Now we are ready to understand the mindset of an entrepreneur. The drive, the need to create something that no one else understands.

Finally we are ready to commit to classes. Ready to commit to conference and group events. And We are ready to actually follow the advice of or mentors from long past.

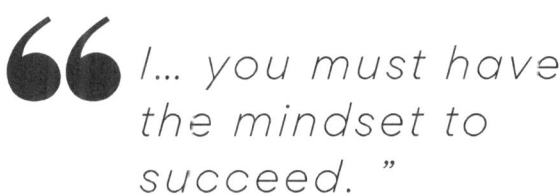

I... you must have the mindset to succeed. "

No longer do we hear the nay-sayers that told us it can't be done. We don't hear those who we have long out grown. No, we now fall into the class that is teaching others to chase their dreams. We are the ones leading the future while still finding our path. So we connect with Key note speakers and hear how they command a room. We take notes from watching shows like Shark Tank on how to seek investors. Our Day job now takes up less of our time as we put everything we have into our dreams.

Everyday we hear one more piece of advice from mentors that don't even know us. People we look up to for answers. Or ones that offered advice long ago that we were not ready to hear. We hear the words that long ago we ignored from our family members and teachers. Words of wisdom we took fro granted from mentors we can no longer reach. Yet it is them we will credit when our dreams become the reality that we see.

For some of my mentors, those who I can call and ask advice from and those who wouldn't know me for the thousands of other followers please see the 22 best coaches for entrepreneurs. There are others who have gotten me here today, but they are the ones who have helped me find my voice.

Yet you ask who is this person to offer advice? Not a name that i hear on the T.v or radio. Not a person who seeks the spotlight.

To you I answer, I am ni tthe one who is meant to be under the microscope of fame. not the one to see out riches and things as a child I have always thought far from my reach. No I am a simple author. A mother who sees the world not as the media paint it but for the truth that is around me. I am nothing more than the person you are now, only have have grown to the mindset of no longer hearing the negitive from those around me.

Grown to over come thigns that most would have been burried under. My pain has turned to a streangth that I offer freely to those who need it.

Who am i? I am the person I choose to be. The mentor that some are ready to hear. The one driven to help where I can. That my friends is who I am. But I would never have gotten here if not for my mentors.

Words of wisdom spoken long ago finally being understood.. dreams I once thought out of my reach now here in the palms of my hand. All because of those I follow and those who i strive to be in the compnay with.

For my mentors thank you.

Photo by: Chyenne Lyons

ROCK YOUR AUDIENCE!
with Rocky Romanella

In this edition, as you prepare to emerge from the pandemic, I would like to discuss two critical factors for success:

- The Leadership Competencies and Skills of your team
- The Organizational Agility of your team post pandemic

The Leadership Competencies and Skills of your team

1. A good way of assessing and visualizing your team's leadership competency is by building a competency profile that you can use by individual to assess their strengths, weaknesses, and opportunities for growth.

In its simplest form, think of it as:

• What is the issue/opportunity and skills that must be addressed? (Developing vision and purpose) for both the person and the organization.

• How will I get my team aligned and committed? (Gaining organizational commitment)

• How do I turn intent into business results? (Achievement)

• The competency profile describes the "right stuff" the leader must have to get the job done.

2. Competency Profiling and Leadership Behaviors

Competencies are characteristic behaviors associated with strong and effective performance in organizational roles. They are actual, delivered behaviors. When such behaviors are delivered, they result in good organizational outcomes. They are also the behaviors that distinguish superior performance from threshold performance.

3. A leadership competency profile should be anchored to the key organizational opportunities and challenges. Competencies are "named" and then defined with a set of behavioral indicators.

The Organizational Agility of your team post pandemic

In the case of Organizational Agility, the example may be: Our company has several challenges as it pertains to the current business landscape post pandemic:

Challenges:

1. New technology and especially, disruptive technology is driving the industry to entirely new platforms for both products and service and we were not strong in e-commerce.

2. Competitors with new and better products are eating into our market share by as much as 25% per year.

3. Cost of sales are rising.

4. Talent defection is becoming a serious issue post pandemic.

5. A climate survey has revealed deteriorating morale across the company.

6. Customer complaints had doubled within a space of nine months.

Company strengths:

1. Sitting on a substantial cash reserve due to the measure we took

2. High recurring revenue from a broad-based customer portfolio

3. Brand strength — high

4. Fixed costs — lowest in the industry

5. Strong dealer network

" For more on these critical topics in preparation for your successful emergence post pandemic
visit:
http://www.3sixtymanagementservices.com.

Pick up a copy of Tighten The Lug Nuts where many of these thoughts and concepts are built out further,
https://tightenthelugnuts.com/.

Lessons from the book
Tighten The Lug Nuts

TightenTheLugNuts.com

" There is no elevator to success. You have to take the stairs. It is the hard work we do today that will get us through tomorrow. "
Rocky Romanella

Visit the Leadership Library at
https://www.3sixtymanagementservices.com/rockys-podcast/.

VISIT OUR INFORMATION LIBRARY:

View all of our Keynote Speaking videos here, or watch a short sample from the library here.

Watch a video on our consulting services here.

Rocky was recently interviewed by a British TV outlet, BV-TV, for the Achiever Leader Show. You can view that video at the homepage at 3SixtyManagementServices.com.

Much more is available at these links:

Virtual Keynotes - https://www.3sixtymanagementservices.com/motivational-speaker/
Virtual Meetings - https://www.3sixtymanagementservices.com
Virtual Training - https://www.3sixtymanagementservices.com/training/
Traditional Consulting - https://www.3sixtymanagementservices.com/consulting/

Much more is available at these links:

Podcasts Library - https://www.3sixtymanagementservices.com/rockys-podcast/
Videos Library- https://www.3sixtymanagementservices.com/youtube-videos/
Our book, Tighten The Lug Nuts: The Principles of Balanced Leadership - https://www.3sixtymanagementservices.com/book-tighten-the-lug-nuts/
List of 23 Leadership Competencies - https://www.3sixtymanagementservices.com/
Coaches Corner - https://www.3sixtymanagementservices.com/category/leadership-training/

" Contact Rocky today to lead your strategy sessions, rapid rebuild plans and communications with your teams. He is available virtually today and live in the not-too-distant future.

Contact Rocky at rockyromanella@gmail.com,
or call 610-322-0720

EMAIL ROCKY TODAY

For additional information visit our website:
https://www.3sixtymanagementservices.com/

submissions@trientpress.com

> The worst enemy to creativity is self-doubt.
>
> — SYLVIA PLATH

Trient Press

Quit doubting yourself. You've got what it takes.

Give us a call today.

~Now accepting all genres~

ADVICE

Dear Holly K

BY: HOLLY K

THE NAKED TRUTH

By: HOLLY K BROOKS
Holly K Brooks is an Intuitive Psychic, Spiritual Life Counselor, Teacher of Life Skills, Podcast Personality and contributing writer to many publications. If you are wrestling with a challenge that needs an answer, please send your questions to Trient Press Magazine.....

TRIENT PRESS MAGAZINE

Dear Holly K

Last week, my 13-year-old daughter came home with a puppy. A St. Bernard puppy. The financial expense is ok. The tasks of feeding, walking, training & cleaning up after him is not ok with me. This could either be a great lesson in responsibility or a total disaster. "Animal mother lover?"

Dear Mother lover, Ahh the delight of having children. Even though those dogs become very large; I say, give her a chance. 13 is a perfect age to give her that "huge" responsibility. Not to mention the benefits of having something to do with all those age-appropriate raging hormones. Rome (good name for the dog) wasn't built in a day; with gentle guidance and a check list; give her 2 months, gentle guidance & a check list. You fiddle while Rome flourishes. Buy a lot of food!

Dear Holly K

• I am a single father...My dating life is spotty at best. My friends suggested a dating site. I have heard of the perils, cat fishing, & lies that can be part of this method. I'm lonely, but hesitant. Advice please!

Daddy Dearest, Let's look at is this way; you are wrestling with fear; valid and understandable. Be aware that great things happen outside of your comfort zone. Be smart, be vigilant. Do not give out any personal information. Every dating site has rules, read and abide by them. It is a new world, join us. Sending you positive dating Mojo. Let me know how it goes. You never know, until you try.

Dear Holly K

- **Dear Holly K**

My husband leaves every Wednesday at 8pm. He returns at 10pm. He tells me he is at his brother's house. However, his brother goes to an AA meeting that night, no one is supposed to know. I feel he is having an affair with my sister-in-law. What do I do?

Dear Sweet girl, it occurs to me that your husband is attending those meetings with your brother on the D.L. You need to have a "sit down" with hubby and ask him point blank. Trust me, you will know by his face, tone and body language. Auntie Hol' has very strong feelings that you are letting your imagination get the better of you. Love & trust are key. Let me know how it goes.

Explore, Thrive, Expand

By: Raine Dalrymple
Inspired Sacred Soul

How do we navigate a learning curve that will encourage us to fully embrace our Soul and everything that our soul has to offer, first to higher self knowledge and secondly in allegiance to our called purpose. Our desire is to become more and in our delayed spiritual progression, only produces more of what has been in the past. So, it is within the concept of explore, thrive and expand, that we become attuned to create a greater world and a New Earth.

We explore the possibility of creating a New Earth, by opening up into an awareness through mindfulness. By visiting with our thoughts in a contemplative state, we move into a space of calm receptivity. We turn our energy inward to the integral intimacy of our spirit. We rest in quieted serenity with our breath and it is there that the magic of our Soul's acceleration, is drawn into connection with a superpower. It is in this cosmic realm, we connect with a thriving source, as we begin to grasp a glimpse of elation, carrying us eloquently into Universal expansion. This Universal expansion holds keys to assist us on our journey. It is guidance that contributes to our own progression, as well as in the benevolence for our earth and others, thoughts, ideas and exacting revelation. This newfound expansion transcends anything we will ever know on an earth plane level. It is the mind of consciousness.

In the promotion of becoming conscious, we interconnect with Infinite Intelligence that transcends the wealth of all worlds. Our burdens become lighter, our hopes imaginable, as we dance with an inner knowledge, that transforms all things. When we give our soul permission to tap into all possibility, we generate a progression into intelligence that pivots transformation. Entertaining the wealth of this transformation, in every possible gift for ourselves, to each other and within the world dynamic, we overturn misalignment and increase life's flow. Each time we return to the real world in real time, we are awakened to the synchronicities in the flow that accompanies our newfound awareness.

Our soul is no longer divided, as we continue to explore, thrive and expand in unison with Infinite Intelligence that guides. We are home.

Dove & Dragon Radio

Each episode a new story to tell

Airs on Iheart Radio, Spotify
Google Podcasts
Amazon Music
and YouTube

Trient Press

RESOURCES FOR NEW AUTHORS

WRITERS AND AUTHORS:

Informative Industry Information Sources (Self-Pub and Traditional)

- The Future of Ink
https://thefutureofink.com/

- Writing On the Ether
https://www.janefriedman.com/blog/

- Gutsy Indie Publishers (FB Group)
https://www.facebook.com/groups/387267894630479/

- ALLi (Alliance of Independent Authors)
https://www.allianceindependentauthors.org/

- A Newbie's Guide To Publishing
http://jakonrath.blogspot.com/2010/04/newbies-guide-to-publishing-book.html

- The Book Designer
https://www.thebookdesigner.com/

- Let's Get Visible
https://davidgaughran.com/

- Bookbub Partners
https://insights.bookbub.com/

- Reedsy (New to publishing? This resource list will help!)
https://blog.reedsy.com/

- Jane Friedman's The Hot Sheet
https://hotsheetpub.com/

Platform, Marketing & Promotion Advice:

Kristen Lamb: We Are Not Alone
https://authorkristenlamb.com/

Pro-Blogger
https://problogger.com/

Jane Friedman
https://www.janefriedman.com/

The Creative Penn
https://www.thecreativepenn.com/blog/

Molly Greene
http://molly-greene.com/

WHW Marketing Posts That May Help:

The FAR Marketing Method: Angela's strategy for relationship-based marketing and why it works
https://writenowcoach.com/far_marketing/

Creative Book Launches That Command Attention: A breakdown for hosting a successful event
https://writershelpingwriters.net/2013/11/creative-book-launches-that-command-attention/

Asking For Online Exposure: The do's and don'ts when approaching top bloggers for visibility
https://writershelpingwriters.net/2013/09/need-online-exposure-asking-bloggers-for-help/

Hand Selling: How Savvy Are You? Observations on what works and what doesn't
https://writershelpingwriters.net/2013/09/hand-selling-your-book-how-savvy-are-you/

RESOURCES FOR ENTREPRENEURS

The 22 Best Business Coaches to Follow in 2021

- **Antonio T. Smith, Jr.**
CEO - ATS Jr Companies, Mindset Mentor, Podcast Host, best selling author
https://www.instagram.com/theatsjr/

- **Brad Balzar**
Performance Coach, Global Speaker, Top Rated #1 Book for entrepreneurs, Founder of Capital School
https://www.instagram.com/bradblazar

- **Daymond John**
Shark, Brand Consultant , Best selling author, Motivational Speaker
https://www.instagram.com/thesharkdaymond/

- **Kevin Harrington**
Entrepreneur, Pioneer, & Business Shark, author, keynote speaker
https://www.instagram.com/realkevinharrington/

- **Erin Henry**
Australian Motivator and Digital Entrepreneur
https://www.instagram.com/erinmayhenry/

- **Barry Moltz**
Entrepreneur, Author, Motivational Speaker, and Small Businesses
https://www.instagram.com/barrymoltz/

- **Melinda Emerson**
Small Business Expert
https://www.instagram.com/smallbizlady/

- **Sheri Kaye Hoff**
Business Coaching and Mindset Expert
https://www.instagram.com/sherikhoff/

- **Dan Sullivan**
Founder and President of the Strategic Coach Inc.
https://www.instagram.com/dr_dan_sullivan/

- **Brad Sugars**
Founder and CEO of Action Coach
https://www.instagram.com/bradleysugars/

- **Loren Fogelman**
Spokesperson and Business Coach
https://www.instagram.com/loren.fogelman/

RESOURCES FOR ENTREPRENEURS

The 22 Best Business Coaches to Follow in 2021

- **Robert Viney,**
Business Coach, and Entrepreneur
https://www.instagram.com/prestigebusinesscoaching

- **Paul Martinelli**
Belief Leadership
https://www.instagram.com/martinelli_paul/

- **Rieva Lesonsky**
Columnist on Small Business Trends and Coach
https://www.instagram.com/rievaandbrian/

- **Karen Skidmore**
Business Coach, Marketing Mentor, and Profit Catalyst
https://www.instagram.com/karenskidmore/

- **Lizzie Moult**
Marketing and Mindset Mentor, Podcast Host, and Founder of Business Basecamp
https://www.instagram.com/lizzie_moult/

- **Natalie Heeley**
UK Network Marketer Business Coach
https://www.instagram.com/rwmgroup/

- **Alan S. Adams**
Award-Winning Business Coach, Bestselling Author
https://www.instagram.com/alansadams/

- **Carrie Green**
Entrepreneur Business Coach
https://www.instagram.com/iamcarriegreen/

- **Kayla Brissi**
Marketing Strategies, Bestselling Author
https://www.instagram.com/kaylabrissi/

- **Bekka Prideaux**
New Perspective Business Coach
https://www.instagram.com/bekkaprideaux/

- **Lorraine Robles**
Genius Finder Business Coach
https://www.instagram.com/lorrainerobles_/

Podcasts Every Entrepreneur Should listen to

The Tim Ferriss Show
https://tim.blog/podcast/

It Will Come Quickly
https://www.youtube.com/c/TheATSJr/featured

StartUp | Gimlet - Gimlet Media
https://gimletmedia.com

Online Marketing Made Easy Podcast with Amy Porterfield
https://www.amyporterfield.com/amy-porterfield-podcast/

Youpreneur
https://youpreneur.com/podcast/

Need help getting booked?

Match Maker FM
https://www.matchmaker.fm/

Command Your Brand
https://commandyourbrand.com/book-a-call-google/

Perfect Podcast Guest
https://perfectpodcastguest.com/

Pod Chaser
https://www.podchaser.com/pro

Podcast Bookers
https://podcastbookers.com/

Pitch Podcasts
https://pitchpodcasts.com/

Radio Guest List
https://www.radioguestlist.com/blog_index.html

Podcast Guest
https://podcastguests.com/

Find Radio Guests
https://www.findradioguests.com/

The Oak Mont Group, LLC
https://www.theoakmontgroupllc.com/how-to-become-a-guest-on-a-podcast/

ENTREPRENEURS HELPING ENTREPRENEURS   Trient Press Magazine

From Trient Press

Change your mindset. Change your life.

TRIENT PRESS

Magazine

Trientrepreneur

A Trient Press Magazine for Authors & Entrepreneurs

Issue 1| April 2021 $10.99

AUTHOR INTERVIEWS

Interviews with new authors, discuss their writing

ENTREPRENEUR HELP

Entrepreneur guidance for premier sources in everything small business.

COMFORT

GUEST ARTICLES

Have something to share with Authors and Entrepreneurs submit a story to: info@trientmagaize.com

INTERVIEWS

For radio interviews there is a fee: https://calendly.com/mlruscsak-ceo/30min

For free printed interviews Contact Info@trientpress.com

www.ingramcontent.com/pod-product-compliance
Lightning Source LLC
Chambersburg PA
CBHW041059070526
44579CB00002B/11